Love Your Story

Let God Define Your Story To Be The Champion You Were Meant To Be

Linda A Olson

#1 International Amazon Bestseller

Love Your Story
Let God Define Your Story To Be The Champion You Were Meant To Be

Copyright © 2020 Linda A Olson.

Cover design by 100Covers.com
Formatted by FormattedBooks.com

ISBN: 978-0-9819014-4-2

———❧❦❧———

…to all the wonderful friends, leaders,
entrepreneurs, authors, speakers,
business owners and ministry workers I
have rubbed shoulders with.
It's because of your influence and impact in my life that
I am who I am today.

———❧❦❧———

My Gift To You

....

In *Love Your Story*, you will discover:

- How to grasp the true gift of reflection; the mirror to see your true self
- A simple pathway to your true identity, who you are in Christ
- How true champions are created
- Strengths you didn't even know you had
- The favor on your life
- Practical tools to rise above every challenge and soar

Gifts/Tools

In addition to what I just mentioned I have included a number of gifts and tools to help you *love your story*. If your heart is open and you follow the simple tools in this practical book you will learn what it means to *love your story*. What is more important than loving yourself at this time is whether you are becoming the Champion you were called to be.

No one has a story just like you. Your story is unique. It is the greatest gift you have been given. That is what sets you apart as an individual. Loving your story is what allows you to rise above your circumstances regardless of how painful they are. You need to know you are made for something more. You were created to be a champion.

You may be thinking, that is fine for you to say but you haven't walked in my shoes. You are right, I haven't. However, the one thing I have learned through my forty-five year journey to love my story is there is nothing too big for God to heal. Through my journey, I learned lessons and gathered tools that allowed me to rise above the darkest moments in my life. In this book, I wanted to share some of those tools with you so hopefully you, too, can appreciate your value and begin to embrace the unique and wonderful person you are.

Brene Brown says it well, *When we deny the story it defines us. When we own the story, we can write a brave new ending.*

A significant part of loving your story is owning your story. I pray that you will embrace the tools within this book and find a deeper level of healing than anything you have ever experienced.

Following My Gift to You, I have included a Pdf on "Owning Your Story Before It Owns You. When you follow the five simple steps outlined in this Pdf you will have a better understanding of what it means to own your story. Better yet, you can enjoy a freedom you never thought was possible.

In addition to the tools within the book, I am offering six additional resources valued at over fifteen hundred dollars in the back of the book. All of these were created for one reason; to help you love your story. Every time you step closer to loving your story it is like getting a promotion from God. No one cares as much as He does. Remember, He is the One that defines your story so you can become the Champion you were called to be.

The additional Gifts/tools include:

1. **Breakthrough: Five Simple Steps to Letting Go of the Past**. Following these five simple steps will guide you to breakthrough. You will discover a new freedom you may not have known was even possible. This one tool alone is priceless. For more watch Linda's TEDx talk https://www.youtube.com/watch?v=skMnvS48MsY and discover how Linda learned to let go of her past after a tragedy that nearly crushed her life. After watching the TEDx talk, I ask that you kindly leave a review. I would love to hear what impacted you.

2. **Defeating Your Goliath.** This simple tool can bring breakthrough in as little as 7 days or less.

3. **Champions Dream Big.** This powerful one-year program will show you how simple breakthroughs, done consistently, can lead to a powerful transformation. You will enjoy fun 5-day Challenges, accountability and more abundance than you ever dreamed possible.

4. **Five Simple Steps Using Story to Attract more Customers.** This is a powerful tool that can be used in the marketplace or in ministry to help you discover what you are really offering. Another helpful resource is participating in our story community. To do so, ask to join the private community of Amazing Storytellers facebook group, (the one with the butterfly), and begin to share your stories.

5. **Create A Story That Transforms.** In only 5 days you can go from not being sure you have a story to creating a transformational story. This 5-day challenge is valued at $197 but I am offering it to you for only $17. Email linda@wealththroughstories.com to find out when the next challenge is offered.

6. **Wealth Through Stories LIVE, Story Retreat** is two full days of experiencing story. You will discover how to find, create and tell your story in 2 minutes or less. Better yet, we will show you how you can transform someone's life through story and impact more people that you ever imagined. My goal is to exceed your expectations. Inspirational, Experiential, Transformational. The Retreat is valued at $997. Sign up while the price is reduced and enjoy a $100 coupon (my gift to you) to make it affordable for everyone.

Guest Speakers: Included in our Story Retreat are special Guest Speakers. Although they may vary, two of our most popular guests are:

Barb Marshall, TV host and producer has found it her mission to help ordinary people take their extraordinary story to reach millions. Barb trusts God to provide for her as she carries out His mission. Her show live streams to over 161 countries, impacting millions.

Cindy Chatham, former Executive Editor for Heartbeat Magazine, enjoys working with authors to make their manuscripts come alive in crisp, clear, and concise ways.

Click here to download your FREE pdf,
wealththroughstories.com/own-your-story/

Own Your Story Before It Owns You

5 Steps to Freedom

Wealth Through Stories
"IMPACTING MILLIONS THROUGH STORY"

by Linda A. Olson

Acknowledgments

....

"Thank you to each of you who have been part of my journey throughout the writing of the book and all the way to publication."

Editor & Friend, Cindy Chatham. Your dedication, help, and patience to bring clarity and excellence to my work means more to me than you will ever know. Thank you for believing in me.

My Mentors. Scott Allen, Chandler Bolt & the team from Self-publishing school, with your excellent work, support, and resources

100 Covers and Formatted Books who patiently worked with me. Thank you for your attention to detail, dedication & excellent work.

Prayer Partners; Margaret Buhler (Aunt Margaret), Rick Bergen, Carl Dyck and Teri White. Your dedication to praying for me and our family, and your love, support, and faithfulness mean more than words can express.

Rick Olson, Spouse, Best Friend, Business Partner. For your countless hours to assist me with my website, design work, and awesome support. Your support means more than you know.

Thank you!

What Others Are Saying

···

Linda Olson has done a masterful job at making what tends to be a mystery for most, a very achievable and valuable reality for us all. Linda truly provides incredible clarity, empowerment and attainability to "Love Your Story"! With an emphasis on intentionality, this book is inspirational as well as motivational—challenging us and equipping us to be all our Creator empowered and designed us to be. If you are a coach, trainer or consultant, having this invaluable tool in your toolbox will exponentially help your clients achieve more in their lives, business' and careers than they ever dreamt of achieving...it's certainly in mine!

—Bill Pavelich, CPC, CEO and
Founder at PerspectivEdge, Charlotte NC,
"Shaping Strategies for Success"

"Oh the thrill of getting a fresh grip on your life—with renewed hope and energy flowing in you, hour by hour!

That is exactly what you will experience as you read Linda's powerful insights! You have been created for a very unique purpose. Open these pages and discover how to live the life you are meant to live, with meaning and joy!"

—Glenna Salsbury, Professional Speaker,
Author of *The Art of the Fresh Start*
glennasalsbury.com

I met Linda Olson a few years ago at a Christian Women in Media Association National Conference. She served on a panel and I was impressed with her wisdom and knowledge on how to best present yourself in one-minute for a media interview and as an author and platform speaker. One of the qualities I admire about Linda is her transparency. Her writing style is engaging and her gift of encouragement is contagious. Through her journey in life and as a woman of prayer, I especially admire Linda for giving God and God alone the glory. You will want to read and share this book with many people.

—Sharon Hill, Prayer Coach,
Conference Speaker and Author of the
OnCall Prayer Journal. www.OnCallPrayer.org

If you are feeling like anything but a "Champion," this book was written for you! For over three decades I have taught people how to eliminate physical and digital clutter, emphasizing that "Clutter is Postponed Decisions®," but in recent years I have become passionate about the reality that if you eliminate the spiritual and emotional clutter in your life, the physical and digital will fall away. This book addresses that very issue. Thank you, Linda!

—Barbara Hemphill, Founder,
Productive Environment Institute

A master teacher once told his student teachers, "If you want to get across an important concept, get it down to its lowest common denominator." Linda Olson has done just that in her book, *Love Your Story.* Servants of the Lord must know wholeheartedly in their mind and spirit just who they are in Christ Jesus in order to fulfill all that God has for them. Gifted communicator and teacher, Linda Olson, has wisely deduced for every one of us both real and practical ways to reach our potential and experience a new freedom and zeal to pursue the exciting and God-given dreams that live in our hearts. The Body of Christ desperately needs every member fulfilling their place for the building up of the Church and this book is appropriately timed in is publication for "such a time as this."

—Rev. Gwen Ehrenborg, Pastor;
Living Witnesses Ministries, Founder;
Supporting Women In Ministry International

In this simple yet profound book by Linda Olson, everyone will benefit enormously from truths embodied therein. This book will help you come to terms with the champion you were created to be and begin manifesting that. This book is simply revolutionary as you learn to correct wrong foundations in your belief system and set yourself up for an astronomical transformation. *Love Your Story* is a must read and I counsel you to read it with a pen in hand to write down revelations that will unravel in the process.

—Godlove Ngufor Author of
Empowering Potential:Re-birthing the
African Entrepreneurial Spirit.

Linda Olson's new book *Love Your Story* delivers on its promise to give you tools and techniques to reach your highest potential. Linda not only talks the talk, she walks the walk. With over 45 years of life experience including battling negative and limiting thoughts, Linda speaks from experience with authenticity and grace. She knows what she is talking about and she truly cares about your journey to uncovering the champion that you are. Do yourself a favor. Read this book and then connect with Linda.

—Leslie J. Smith, B.A., LL.B., Oakville, Ontario, Canada.
Lawyer, Small Claims Court Judge, Mediator, Speaker and
Author of *Legal Ease – Essential Legal Strategies to
Protect Canadian Non-Union Employees.*

Linda offers useful and much needed wisdom as she addresses the topic of believing in yourself, in her book, "Love Your Story". If her readers will apply even a few of her 101 Truths to their lives, they will definitely have new, exciting and more powerful life experiences!

—Margie McIntyre, author of Mind
Matters–Change Your Mind, Change Your Life.
www.mindmattersseries.com

"Love Your Story" reveals the simple yet profound truth that you have been created by God to excel in life. Linda Olson's heart is for each person to live a life of their dreams."

—Sue Detweiler, author of
9 Traits of a Life-Giving Mom
www.SueDetweiler.com.

"Love Your Story" will cause you to get to know yourself better. Discover that the champion within (the one you always knew was there) is really there and can come forth. Linda gives tools to unleash you into the champion you were created to be and find out what is keeping that champion locked up inside. I highly recommend this book for anyone ready for transformation.

—Pamela Rohr, author of Blended But Not Broken;
Hope and Encouragement for Blended Families.
www.nouveaulifecoaching.com

In Linda Olson's book, *Love Your Story*, Linda writes from a heart of understanding from her own life experiences and coaching, which comes across in a way that is part testimony, story and practical application. If you want to examine how you see your self, how others see you, and who you are in Christ–your true identity, Linda provides a wonderful blueprint to self-discovery and the inspiration that can take you to the next level, in uncovering the champion within!

—Carol Doyle, Founder of on-line women's magazine,
LivingBetter50.com, Christian Women in Media
(CWIMA), West Coast/Hollywood Regional Director

It is a joy and a privilege to celebrate the victory of Christ Jesus through His words gifted to you because Linda has been obedient to Jesus' calling by writing this book. "Love Your Story" is a rich profound book of encouragement revealing all the incredible gifts and graces that our Lord has given you since birth. As you, the reader, are open to the enlightenment you receive through each word, may you be filled with the joy of your potential, touching, healing and enriching the lives of many along your journey. This book is the beginning of the new you for the glory of our Lord. Linda has remained faithful and may each of you rejoice in loving your story.

> —Carmen Warner-Robbins, CEO, Welcome Home
> Ministries, Chaplain, American Jail Association

Linda's writing is a beautiful blend of scripture and psychology including life-changing principles drawn from spiritual truth and the study of human behavior. This is a much-needed balance for our lives today. I am challenged and encouraged.

> —Rev. Mike L. Harreld,
> M.Div. Chaplainonline, Overcoming Adversity

Linda Olson has systematically laid out for us practical basic truths that took me at least ten years to learn and put into practice. Hours of study of the Word of God, tons of books, stacks of articles, and countless sermons, brought me the information she has covered in one simple book. When we devour this book, daily practice each step and allow it to change our mentality, our growth will be exponential. Accelerate your journey—it won't take you ten years like it did me—grow and mature. Soon you'll see results.

—Diane Gardner, Speaker, Transformation Coach,
Author of *Overcoming the Enemy's Storms*
www.beautifulwomenofGod.org
www.overcomingtheenemysstorms.com

Powerful truth in this book from Linda Olson about embracing your unique God-given gifts! Thank you Linda for sharing your message of faith, action, and letting God lead the way as we walk our champion path. He knows where He needs us…our job is to let Him use us! This book is a guide and partner for the journey.

—*Diane Cunningham*
Founder and President National Association
of Christian Women Entrepreneurs
www.nacwe.org Amazon Best Selling Author of
4 books including "The Inspired Business Toolkit"
and "Rock Bottom is a Beautiful Place"

"Linda has a passion for nurturing and developing leaders to be who God created and called them to be. Her heart beats to serve God and connect others to Him- this book will help you do just that."

—Christie Love, Founder and Executive
Director of LeadHer
www.leadher.org

Linda blossoms at making a difference in women's lives. She has a gift from God to transform the lives of women while helping them find their vision, mission, and purpose. Her unique ability helps women thrive. Linda's devotion, determination and love to help all succeed is apparent. She is an incredible woman of faith who has a huge passion to touch hearts. And she does it effectively.

> —*Barbara Marshall, President Love Your Life Ministries and Founder of Love Life Today, TV producer and TV host of the The Barb Marshall cable access Show, author, and international speaker. www.barbtv.org*

Contents

Foreword

by *Kathleen Mailer*

*H*ave you ever really looked at yourself in the mirror? I don't mean a quick check to see if your personal grooming is adequate for the day, I mean really STUDY the person that stares back at you. This small act can bring up a myriad of emotions.

Many people find this extremely uncomfortable. They feel unattractive, unworthy, hopeless, ashamed, inadequate, stupid. Some even feel guilt, condemnation, incompetence, and self-loathing. They begin to judge themselves by what they see. The negative self-talks become demeaning, attacking, critical, and abusive. How about you? Does this sound familiar? The problem is you don't understand the true gift of reflection.

Once you begin to embrace the simple exercises inside this book, you will find that you can change your perspective. Once that changes everything around you changes. You become 'free' of your *Inner Terrorist*. This is what I lovingly call 'that guy' inside your head that says, "I am not smart enough. I am not good enough. No one understands me." ...Come on! You KNOW who I am talking about here! Once your I.T. is silenced you can begin to see your intrinsic self-worth. You begin to understand your passion, your purpose, and that there is more to your existence than you could ever have known. Your life will begin to unfold as a beautiful butterfly emerging from his cocoon.

Linda Olson, like a true blue friend, holds your hand to comfort you as you walk through the entire process. *Love Your Story* becomes the mirror we need to 'see' the real truth. It is our birthright to be empowered, strong, healthy (emotionally and physically). I believe God's intention for this extraordinary book is to unleash your potential so you can move forward in the pre-ordained plan He has set aside specifically for your life. Now the plans that He has to prosper can be emancipated!

Once you pick up this little gem and begin to reflect on the simple truths about who you are, you will see the beautiful, exquisite, exciting person God created you to be. You will be able to understand your inherent self-respect and the value you bring to the world. You will be able to step forward in faith with your head held high and a song on your heart.

The devil will rue the day he messed with you! I say, 'Let him run! – Look out! – Jesus' disciple is fully armed and ready to go!"

I pray you will find the wholeness in your heart you have been searching for. I guarantee, the novice to a seasoned Christian, you will receive life-altering revelations in this power-packed, award-winning formula.

Isn't it time to take a stand?

—Warmly,
Kathleen Mailer
Kathleen D. Mailer, is THE *International Business Evangelist*, Creator of "A Book Is Never A Book" Boot Camp, Author of 37 books including, "Prepare To Prosper, Taking Your Business To A HIGHER LEVEL"

Preface

a note from Linda Olson

I n 1966, I faced a devastating time of my life, and I didn't know if I would ever recover. Today I look back in awe, recognizing what only God could do. He not only put me on my feet, carried me, and brought healing, but He also showered me with His gifts and anointing beyond anything I could have imagined.

I have a heart of gratitude to Jesus Christ who has made all this possible. A few months prior to the idea of this book, He inspired me with the words, *"With God all things are possible."* They were the same words the angel Gabriel gave Mary the mother of Jesus. I knew this would be a big year but had no idea what was in store. Little did I know that this book would be birthed in less than seven months after He gave me the idea to write it. Then with the help of the Holy Spirit, I committed myself to follow through with each step of the process. He gave me the words when I had nothing left to say. He was strong when I was weak. He was there every day, every moment.

In the process, He showed me that I am the voice to empower others with their voice. I am both humbled and honored to be used by Him for such a time as this. There is nothing I desire more but that He would be glorified through this work. My prayer is that this text would not only touch but also transform millions of lives. It offers a simple pathway for the most important thing we need to know: who we are in Christ. When we embrace our true identity, and love our story, we will break through every barrier.

Oswald Chambers said, "*Simplicity is the secret to seeing things clearly.*" I pray that through this simple book, you will allow God to define your story and become the champion you were meant to be. Regardless of where you are in life, God will give you clarity, strength, and courage to write a brave, new ending. He created you and desires for you to love your story. When you do, He will have opportunities for you that you cannot even imagine.

Part 1

DISCOVERING
MY STRENGTHS

Chapter 1

How I See Myself

....

It was a beautiful late September afternoon. I sat under the big maple tree with golden leaves all around me. Three weeks after arriving at college, I was contemplating an assignment to write a paper on my personal strengths and weaknesses. It was a day when I could have enjoyed the beauty surrounding me. Instead I stared at a blank piece of paper. Well, it was not completely blank because I had already written a long list of weaknesses, but somehow I could not think of my personal strengths. I had not excelled in any sports—or anything else, for that matter. I was just an ordinary, hard-working farm girl. There was nothing special about me. Anyone could do what I did. I felt so insecure around the talented students at college. In fact, I wondered what I was doing there and if I could even handle the academics. Worse yet, my self-worth had been tied to my performance.

Just then I watched someone drive away from campus. I remember thinking, *If they stop and ask me if I want a ride home, I just might say, 'Yes'.* Then I reconsidered. What would life be like if I went back to where I grew up, to the little farming community three hundred miles away? After only a few moments, I realized only family remained there for me. It was a great place to grow up, but at this time in my life no one in my hometown would challenge me intellectually, empower me to dream, or give me the emotional support that would allow me to blossom into more than I could imagine. So, after much thought, I somehow mustered the courage to stay at college.

———— ❖ ————

What about you? If you had to write a paper listing *your* strengths and weaknesses, what would you write about? Transformation doesn't happen unless you take action.

After every chapter in this book is an assignment. Take the time to actually *do* each one. The exercise will be invaluable in moving you forward in your growth. Gail Sheehy, journalist, lecturer, and author of the book *Passages* says, "If we don't change we don't grow. If we don't grow we are not really living." Are you ready to grow?

Let's get started.

ASSIGNMENT 1

List the negative names someone has called you or you have called yourself in the past.

1. _____

2. _____

3. _____

4. _____

5. _____

6. _____

7. _____

8. _____

Now review each name. Consider if it is something that you have overcome. If you still believe the name, write B for "believe" after the corresponding number below. If you have overcome the negative name, cross it out and next to it, write the positive name.

For example: Defeated crossed out, Free; Fearful crossed out, Loved, Hopeless crossed out, Hopeful.

To take this a step further, write out each name again. Now cross it out and write a scripture verse next to it. For example, I

Can't, crossed out. I CAN, "I can do all things through Christ who strengthens me." Philippians 4:13

1. _____

2. _____

3. _____

4. _____

5. _____

6. _____

7. _____

8. _____

The number one question asked around the world is, "Who am I?" At every stage in life a person asks that question one way or another. A two-year old explores his boundaries and discovers who he is in infancy. As he grows and eventually moves into his pre-teen years, he discovers the influence of friends, and changing values help shape who he is. As a teenager caught between childhood and adulthood, he tries to sort out where he belongs, who his friends are, and how to relate to the opposite sex. In his twenties, a young man considers major life decisions such as marriage and career, while still asking the same question, "Who am I?" Often another question follows: "What do I want to do in life?" These questions and decisions continue through marriage, having children, facing the empty nest, and into retirement.

A newscaster recently repeated the words of a mother who just lost her son, "Without my son, I don't know who I am."

A woman, married many years, commented at her husband's funeral, "I don't know who I am."

Your response to the question, "Who am I?" makes up your identity. It is often wrapped around special people in your life, social status, or even your day-to-day performance.

Messages related to your self-worth may be confusing. You may think that if only you were given the opportunity to do something special—something heroic—then others would take notice, and you would be important. That is what I believed growing up. Unfortunately, that expectation results in building your identity on a false foundation.

Peter Vidmar, a former Olympic silver and gold medalist in gymnastics said, "To be an Olympic Champion, you only have to work out two times: when you feel like and when you don't feel like it." That doesn't just apply to Olympic champions. It applies to you as well. You cannot be a champion or impact other through your story without doing the work.

Can you imagine attempting to participate in the Olympics and never having practiced? That is exactly what happens when you desire great opportunities, when you want to become a hero, yet are not willing to develop your own character. And character is often built through a daily walk of mundane tasks. The real champion faithfully does the task before him day in and day out, facing the challenges and remaining positive.

The truth is: you *are* important. And what you *do* is a reflection of who you *are*. Nothing you can do or say makes you more valuable today than you were yesterday; more valuable than the day you were born. All you have to do is believe it.

I know it is one thing to hear these words and quite another to receive the message inwardly. Often people spend time and energy trying to be someone else instead of just enjoying who they are. Oscar Wilde, an Irish writer and poet, says it so well, "Be yourself. Everyone else is already taken."

Norman Vincent Peale, the man known for positive thinking, said, "People become really quite remarkable when they start thinking that they can do things. When they believe in themselves they have the first secret of success."

It all starts with knowing who you are and believing in yourself.

A few years ago, when my husband and I were on vacation, we visited our favorite grocery store *Trader Joe's*. A van pulled up in front of the store. The female driver exited the van, walked around the front of the vehicle, and opened the slider door to pull down a ramp. In moments two young girls wheeled down the ramp in motorized wheelchairs. Both girls, afflicted with cerebral palsy, seemed to be excited about grocery shopping with their mother, the driver of the van. Rick and I heard them laughing and giggling as they went up one aisle and down another. I glanced over just in time to see a handsome young employee of the store place a bouquet of flowers in each of their carts. He said to one of the girls, "Since it is your birthday today, besides the bouquet of flowers I would like to give you a bouquet of balloons."

Then he walked over to the manager's station to announce on the intercom, "We would like everyone to come to the front of the store and help us sing, 'Happy Birthday'. Today is Amy's eleventh birthday!"

We all gathered around the young girls and sang a hearty "Happy Birthday". Amy smiled from ear to ear. She was so excited. This young employee not only exceeded Amy's shopping-day expectations, he also exceeded mine. I knew Amy would never forget the kindness she was given that day.

A year later, Rick and I again were vacationing in the same area and we stopped by the same *Trader Joe's*. "If that young man is still working here," I told my husband, "I would like to ask him a few questions." Sure enough, after talking with the manager, I spied the kind employee. He was bagging groceries. I briefly asked if I may speak with him. He immediately asked if he was in trouble. Chuckling, I told him he wasn't but that I did want to ask him about an incident in the store the year before.

He clearly remembered the entire scene. I asked if he knew the girls. "Never saw them before, never saw them again."

Quite surprised, I said, "Really? So now I'm very curious. How did you know it was Amy's birthday?"

At that point, he looked a bit embarrassed and replied in a low tone, "Well, you never know what you're going to overhear when you sort the fruits and vegetables."

I smiled. "The kindness you showed that day was remarkable; you are a champion." I handed him a copy of my book and said, "Your story didn't make it into my first book, but it will make it into my next book."

He was so excited he hardly knew what to do. He politely asked, "Is it okay to give you a hug?"

"Absolutely!" I replied.

He gave me the biggest bear hug and said, "You just made my day."

I smiled and returned the hug saying, "Thank you. You just made my year."

It seemed so simple. This young man saw an opportunity to encourage someone and, by taking action, he left a positive memory for a lifetime. It's a great reminder that every day there are opportunities to be champions. Dale Carnegie, the famous author of *How to Win Friends and Influence People,* said, "You have it easily in your power to increase the sum total of this world's happiness now. How? By giving a few words of sincere appreciation to someone who is lonely or discouraged. Perhaps you will forget tomorrow the kind words you say today, but the recipient may cherish them over a lifetime."

You are blessed so you can bless others. Edwin Elliot, a mathematician, said, "By being yourself, you put something wonderful into the world that was not there before."

You never know the impact you have on others.

As you consider the messages that have impacted your life, I encourage you to stop and meditate on what you have just read and how it applies to your life. Join me in a prayer for you. As you pray the prayer below, fill in the blank with your name. You may note that sometimes I use him and sometimes her. Just use what is appropriate for you.

Dear Heavenly Father,

We thank you for your awesome love for us. I know how much you love _____.

Please help her to grasp your love. Bring to mind the areas in her life that still need healing. You hear the cry of her heart. Help _____ not to fear negative thoughts or emotions, but rather help her to bring them to you so you can bring healing. For you have said in your Word, "For God has not given us a spirit of fear, but of power and of love and of a sound mind." (2 Timothy 1:7 NKJV). As _____ brings each negative message to you, embrace her with your power, your love, and your sound mind. And we say thank you. Thank you for your care about every detail in _____'s life.

In Jesus' name,
Amen.

Chapter 2

How a Champion
Exhibits Character

∙∙∙

The path to developing a healthy identity is really quite simple. You may ask, "If it's so simple, why are so many men and women stuck in unhealthy relationships? Why are they working at jobs or careers they don't like? Why are they simply unhappy, always looking for someone or something to give them greater fulfillment?"

Yes, I said simple, but I didn't say easy. Let's take a closer look.

What makes some people thrive and enjoy success at every turn when a sibling, having grown up in the same environment with the same parents, goes through life barely surviving? Much of it has to do with personal belief systems. Basing personal belief on a solid foundation of truth makes all the difference. Examples of foundations based on error may be what others say about you, or perhaps what you were told in your childhood. Everything we do—the friendships we make, the careers we invest in, the marriage partners we choose—is based on who we are. You may have heard the phrase, "Like attracts like." This could mean that, in choosing a spouse, you will likely choose someone on a similar emotional level as you are. If you choose relationships or jobs that take you down rather than help you go forward, perhaps you might take a look at the foundational issues. These areas are prime targets for growth. Take a look at the strengths and abilities you have, and then strive forward to address areas that hold you back.

A speaker once shared how every time he wanted to step forward into something new he felt an overwhelming fear. The fear caused him to step backward instead of going forward. Eventually he learned that a certain amount of fear is a natural response to stepping into new territory. So then, instead of retreating from fear, he learned how to face fear in order to go forward.

This is how champions are created. Champions persevere through whatever challenges lie ahead as they follow their passions. As your story changes by persevering through the challenges in your life, your life will impact others through story.

You may not believe you are a champion. But if I spent an hour with you, I know we would discover times in your life when you unknowingly portrayed the traits of a champion. I know I could ask any of your children or grandchildren (if you have them), "What is special about your Mom (or Dad)?" and they would tell me without hesitation. But we may not see those same champion-like qualities in ourselves. Why? Because we may receive many negative messages daily that discount the positive messages that come along. We think "what we don't know won't hurt us".

It's time to uncover the truth.

Self-esteem, or personal worth, is derived from three major sources.

The first source is your own viewpoint, how you see yourself. Yet you may not know how to respond if I asked you that very question, "How do you see yourself?" So, to help you with that response, here is a simple exercise that will clarify how you see yourself.

Nearly one hundred character qualities are listed. Go through the list, marking each quality with a number: strong (4 or 5), average (3), weak (1 or 2), or does not apply (0). Be honest. This is not a game to see how good you can make yourself look, but rather it is an opportunity to view yourself without pretense.

Dear Heavenly Father,

Thank you for your wisdom. You said in your word that if we lack wisdom, all we need to do is to ask and you will give it generously. We ask now that you provide clarity, wisdom, and insight as _____ considers each trait and how it applies to his or her life. And we thank you.

In Jesus' name,
Amen

WHO AM I?

I believe I am...

—— **Accountable.** I answer to at least one other person for my actions and outcome.

—— **Achievement-oriented.** I aspire to the highest level of excellence.

—— **Alert.** I am keenly aware of my surroundings.

—— **Attentive.** I demonstrate respect by giving undivided attention to others.

—— **Authentic.** I am who I claim to be in honesty and transparency.

—— **Available.** I am flexible to the desires of others.

—— **Balanced.** I make wise use of time and effort in various responsibilities.

—— **Bold.** I demonstrate courage and confidence to do what is right.

—— **Boundary-healthy.** I create reasonable limitations to keep myself safe.

—— **Cautious.** I remain actively alert to protect myself from harm.

—— **Cheerful.** I encourage and uplift others in positive ways.

—— **Committed.** I devote myself to completing what I agree to do.

—— **Compassionate.** I am available physically or emotionally to someone who is hurting.

—— **Competent.** I possess skill, knowledge, and ability to perform at certain standards.

—— **Confident.** I put full trust and belief in the reliability of another person, place, or thing.

—— **Consistent.** I repeatedly follow the same pattern, principles, or system.

—— **Content.** I accept myself, being satisfied with my gifts, talents, abilities, and opportunities.

—— **Courageous.** I stand for what is right even when I am uncomfortable.

—— **Creative.** I think originally, finding new ways to accomplish a goal or task.

—— **Decisive.** I make clear, unwavering choices based on what is right.

—— **Dependable.** I fulfill what I agree to do even when it is inconvenient.

—— **Determined.** I remain highly focused in order to accomplish a specific goal or task.

—— **Diligent.** I make every effort to complete the task at hand.

—— **Discerning.** I use wisdom and intuition to make wise decisions.

—— **Dependable.** I keep my word regardless of changing circumstances.

—— **Efficient.** I produce results in a timely manner with minimal expense and effort.

—— **Enduring.** I balance effort and energy in a long-term commitment.

—— **Enthusiastic.** I express energy, passion, and excitement in whatever I face.

—— **Fair.** I treat people with equality.

—— **Faith-full.** I believe, with unshakeable confidence, in what is not seen.

—— **Faithful.** I follow through with commitments.

—— **Firm.** I set clear boundaries without wavering.

—— **Flexible.** I change course in the midst of unexpected circumstances.

—— **Forgiving.** I let go of offenses, and I do not hold grudges.

—— **Fun.** I love expressing humor; I laugh, I am playful, and I am enjoyable to be around.

—— **Generous.** I give freely of myself through time, talents, and finances.

—— **Gentle.** I respond to others with kindness, care, and love.

—— **Goal-oriented.** I focus on achieving maximum results in a specific area.

—— **Grateful.** I offer a heart of thankfulness and express it through words and actions.

—— **Great.** I demonstrate an extraordinary capacity for achievement.

—— **Growth-oriented.** I invest in personal development and lifelong learning.

—— **Honest.** I am truthful and sincere in all situations.

—— **Honor-giving.** I respect those in leadership because of the authority they represent.

—— **Hopeful.** I believe that my deepest desire will be met regardless of the circumstances.

—— **Hospitable.** I give of myself through food, shelter, or finances.

—— **Humble.** I let go of pride to give of myself without expectation of return.

—— **Independent.** I am free from the influence or control of others; I work on my own terms.

—— **Initiating.** I recognize and do what needs to be done before I am asked to do it.

—— **Integrity-driven.** I remain consistent in word and deed.

—— **Joyful.** I express a deep sense of gratitude, often through song, dance, words, or demeanor.

—— **Kind.** I care gently for others.

—— **Knowledgeable.** I attain understanding with facts, truths, or principles.

—— **Lead-oriented.** I take initiative to guide and direct others towards a particular outcome.

—— **Loving.** I give to others through talents, gifts, words, or actions to benefit others.

—— **Loyal.** I demonstrate faithfulness to do what is right even through difficulty.

—— **Nurturing.** I care for the needs of others.

—— **Obedient.** I do what I have been asked to do to the satisfaction of the one who requested it.

—— **Objective.** I look at any situation without emotional investment or selfish motivation.

—— **Optimistic.** I am confident, hopeful, and positive.

—— **Orderly.** I keep things in an organized fashion for greater efficiency.

—— **Original.** I create new ideas, systems, or platforms from an independent viewpoint.

—— **Passionate.** I have intense emotional excitement towards vision, people, or projects.

—— **Patient.** I am accepting, enduring, and tolerant.

—— **Peaceful.** I demonstrate a sense of quiet and calm; I am at rest with myself and others.

—— **Perfectionistic.** I attain a high standard with attention to details.

—— **Persevering.** I am persistent and diligent despite difficulties, failure, and opposition.

—— **Persuasive.** I influence and guide others to accept a new mindset or viewpoint.

—— **Prayerful.** I commune with God through adoration, confession, thanksgiving, and supplication.

—— **Prosperous.** I flourish, thrive, and succeed in many areas, not only financially.

—— **Punctual.** I value the time of others by being prompt in appointments and deadlines.

—— **Pure.** I keep myself clean and wholesome in word and action.

—— **Purposeful.** I determine to remain focused in order to stay on track.

—— **Reasonable.** I make decisions in practical, realistic, and sensible ways.

—— **Resourceful.** I use whatever is available to create in practical ways.

—— **Respectful.** I esteem others with humility and honor.

—— **Responsible.** I know what to do and do it.

—— **Secure.** I am confident in my own self-worth, in who I am and in my purpose for living.

—— **Self-controlled.** I show appropriate restraint by demonstrating strength of mind and will.

—— **Sensitive.** I attend to the needs of those around me by being thoughtful and caring.

—— **Simplistic.** I keep matters simple and clear, omitting chaos and confusion.

—— **Sincere.** I do what is right genuinely, honestly, and truthfully.

—— **Strong in character.** I maintain personal stability, security, humility, and wisdom.

—— **Structured.** I organize and arrange systems or processes, maintaining routine.

—— **Surrendered.** I yield to authority, appropriately submitting.

—— **Teachable.** I am willing to learn and to be trained.

—— **Team-oriented.** I flourish where I cooperate and contribute on behalf of the group.

—— **Thankful.** I express gratefulness and appreciation.

—— **Thorough.** I approach a task in a full, detailed, and exhaustive way.

—— **Thoughtful.** I show consideration for others through acts of kindness and words.

—— **Tolerant.** I accept others as valuable individuals regardless of their maturity.

—— **Transparent.** I allow others to see the real me; I am authentic and vulnerable.

—— **Truthful.** I share facts or feelings honestly, openly, and straight-forwardly.

—— **Trustworthy.** I follow through; I am dependable, reliable, and truthful.

—— **Understanding.** I comprehend matters with empathy, consideration, and thoughtfulness.

—— **Unstoppable.** I perform at my highest level of ability without restriction.

—— **Vision-minded.** I look at long-term solutions and dreams; I am future-minded.

—— **Vulnerable.** I am open to sharing personal feelings.

—— **Wise.** I respond to situations with insight, knowledge, and understanding.

2. Now review your 4's and 5's and list your top 10 character qualities.

1. _____

2. _____

3. _____

4. _____

5. _____

6. _____

7. _____

8. _____

9. _____

10. _____

3. Review the above list of top ten character qualities and write them again below, listing them in descending order from your greatest strength to your least greatest strength.

1. _____

2. _____

3. _____

4. _____

5. _____

6. _____

7. _____

8. _____

9. _____

10. _____

Chapter 3

How Others See Me

•••

*N*ow, let's take a look at how others see you.

Ask five people who know you well if they could spare about 15-20 minutes to help you.

Email linda@wealththroughstories.com asking for a list of the Character Qualities from Love Your Story. Send the list to each of them asking them to go through the qualities describing you. You may also offer to do it for them if they wish.

Ask them to go through the list and indicate the 5's (your greatest strengths). Then ask them to choose the Top 10 character qualities (from the 5's they marked) that they believe best applies to you. List the Top 10 responses below from each person.

Person #1

1. _____

2. _____

3. _____

4. _____

5. _____

6. _____

7. _____

8. _____

9. _____

10. _____

Person #2

1. _____

2. _____

3. _____

4. _____

5. _____

6. _____

7. _____

8. _____

9. _____

10. _____

Person #3

1. _____

2. _____

3. _____

4. _____

5. _____

6. _____

7. _____

8. _____

9. _____

10. _____

Person #4

1. _____

2. _____

3. _____

4. _____

5. _____

6. _____

7. _____

8. _____

9. _____

10. _____

Person #5

1. _____

2. _____

3. _____

4. _____

5. _____

6. _____

7. _____

8. _____

9. _____

10. _____

Compare the traits you listed about yourself with those on your friends' lists. Having many of the same qualities on both lists indicates you know yourself quite well. It also indicates that you are real and authentic.

I heard a national speaker tell the story of a lady who had Alzheimer's. The speaker visited the lady regularly until she eventually passed away. When he attended the funeral he could not help but notice another woman who was sobbing. Wanting to offer her some comfort, he went to sit next to her. As her crying quieted, he said, "Kathryn must have meant a lot to you."

She said, "Yes. You see, I was her nurse. Every day, when I brought her breakfast, she would say, 'Has anyone ever told you how beautiful you are?' She was the only person who ever made me feel worthwhile."

Unfortunately, once Kathryn died, so did the self-worth of this woman.

Do *you* give someone else the power to decide your worth? In this case, it was a positive message. But many times we allow negative messages we hear from others to decide our worth. They may be messages like, "you are not good enough", "you can never do anything right", "you will never amount to anything", or even "what makes you think you can do that?"

Do these messages sound familiar? If we accept negative messages, we give someone else the power to determine our destiny and to steal our joy. These are the kind of things that keep us stuck. When we stop enjoying life, we also fail to reach our potential.

Another reaction is also negative: you spend your days trying desperately to prove someone else in your life was wrong. This response often leads to a driven life that is based on a false foundation. When you know your true identity, there is no need to prove anything.

Dear Heavenly Father,

Thank you for who you are and for how deeply you care for us. As painful as it may be, I ask that you would reveal lies from the enemy that _____ has accepted, anything that leads to a false foundation. You have said, "You shall know the Truth and the Truth shall set you free." You are the Truth and you, alone, can set us free. Help _____ to release those lies that have kept her in bondage. Thank you for giving us access to Your freedom. Help _____ to know the Truth and enjoy a new freedom as she releases the lies and takes on the truth.

We pray these things in the name of the Lord Jesus Christ and cover them under His blood.

Amen.

Part 2

REACHING HIGHER

Suppose you wanted to purchase a used car. You have the opportunity to speak to either the original owner of the car or a friend of the original owner. Whom would you choose? I'm sure you would want to speak to the original owner, just as I would. If you wanted to purchase new furniture, would you want to speak to the one who designed and built the furniture or to someone who worked for the designer? If possible, the one who created it, right? Why? Simply because the person who could best answer your questions and give you the details would be the original owner of the car or the designer of the furniture.

If you really wanted to know more about yourself, whom would you go to: the One who created you, or someone you have met?

Romans 12:3 (The Msg.) tells us, "*The only accurate way to understand ourselves is by what God is and by what he does for us.*"

Ephesians 1:11 (the Msg.) says, "*It's in Christ that we find out who we are and what we are living for…*"

No one knows us better that the One who created us. If you have a personal relationship with Jesus Christ, your true identity is derived from who you are in Christ, the One who created you. If you do not have a personal relationship with Jesus Christ or if you are not sure you have ever made that decision, I encourage you to go to the back of this book and refer to the section *Becoming Part of a Bigger Family.* You will discover how you can begin that relationship today. It is the most important decision you will ever make.

It all starts with God.

"*For everything, absolutely everything, above and below, visible and invisible, rank after rank of angels—everything got started in him and finds its purpose in him.*" (Colossians 1:16 The Msg.)

Your identity—who you are in Christ—is made up of three major areas: your "belongingness", your worth, and your competence. These three areas that make up your identity are further described by the phrases "Embraced by His Love" (which refers to your belongingness), "Treasured by His Worth" (which refers to your personal worth), and "Competent in His Steps" (which refers to your own competence).

"Embraced by His Love" refers to your belongingness. Another way to say this is your acceptance in Christ. Belongingness is not something to be earned or something to be enjoyed temporarily or even something to be taken for granted. Instead, it is the belief that you are created in His image. All you have to do is believe God sent His only Son to die for you and that He rose again, and ask Him to forgive you for any wrongdoing or sin. In accepting His love, you become a part of His family and thereby belong to Him. You are embraced by His love. (For more detail on this, refer to the section at the end of the book titled *Become Part of a Bigger Family*).

In your earthly family, your belongingness is a gift you are given at birth when you were introduced to your new family. In the same way, belongingness in Christ is a gift you are given at your new birth in Christ when you accept His love for you and ask Him to forgive you for your sins. As you are introduced to others who have also made the decision to follow Jesus Christ, they become your spiritual family.

"Treasured by His Worth" refers to your worth in Christ. Your worth is what gives you your true security. Women, especially, have a great need for security. Therefore the biggest area of struggle, if you are female, may be insecurity. As a society, millions of dollars have been spent on attempts to persuade women to improve their physical appearances. This, of course, is an effort to convince women that their worth (as well as their security and happiness) is derived from society's view of beauty.

Another area of perceived personal worth has to do with personal performance, or attempting to prove that you are important based on your performance.

A third area that is often projected onto personal worth is status among others. Once again, we try to make ourselves look good. The sad part is we believe these false messages. Our worth is *not* based on appearance, performance, or status. Rather, personal worth is based on accepting all aspects of God's love for us.

Here is where the gospel gets up close and personal. If you were the only one in the whole world, Jesus would still have sacrificed Himself for you. It's true! That is the depth of His love for you. And beyond that, He is preparing a place in heaven for us so we can enjoy all of eternity with Him. We are treasured by His worth.

"Competent in His Steps" refers to our competence in Him. Our competence is what gives us true significance.

How often do you focus on performance to give you your worth? This may include the upholding of your responsibilities at home; perhaps it would be the completion of chores during childhood. Today it may be through your job or career or even volunteer work. Since performance is often what you are recognized for, the messages can get confusing.

All of these are good and necessary attributes as we strive towards our greatest potential. The part that gets confusing occurs when we equate our performance to our value. When that happens, it only takes one fall, one accident or "mess-up" to completely dissolve the perception of our worth.

Competence is not based on a sense of confidence. Rather it is depending on the Holy Spirit to work in and through us. Whatever task He has called you to do, He will equip you for it so that you may do it well. You may be familiar with the phrase, "*God does not call the equipped, He equips the called.*" That has to do with our competence in Him.

———— ❧ ————

The following pages reflect 101 truths to a powerful you. They are God's expression of how He sees you and what He has to offer you as part of His family. There is nothing more powerful or more valuable than grasping these truths. If you are a member of God's family, you have access to everything that Christ is. The problem is that you may not believe, or accept, or do not access what is available to you. Many of us are content to remain a victim instead of a victor in Christ. But Jesus Christ is all powerful, and He generously and willingly shares His power with us.

2 Timothy 1:7 NLT says, *For God has not given us a spirit of fear and timidity, but of power, love, and self-discipline.*" He has already given us His power but it is only of value when we apply it. When we grasp the power we have in Christ, we will be able to overcome any obstacle or roadblock that comes our way. Can you imagine the impact you will have on others at that time? They will see your strength, they will see your empowerment, they will see who you really are.

Review the *101 Truths* carefully and put a check in front of the ones that you believe and accept to be true.

Dear Heavenly Father,

We thank you that your love for us is more than we can imagine. As _____ reviews your promises, speak to his heart. May _____ truly be able to grasp in a deeper way than ever before how much you love him. Thank you that these promises are your way of saying, "I love you." We know that nothing will ever change your love for _____.

In Jesus' name,
Amen.

Chapter 4

I Am Embraced
by His Love

•••

*

1. **I am His treasured possession.**

   Out of all the peoples on the face of this earth, the Lord has chosen you to be his treasured possession.

   Deuteronomy 14:2 NIV

*

2. **He offers me the key to His love.**

   This is how God showed His love among us: He sent His one and only Son into the world that we might live through Him.

   I John 4:9 NIV

*

3. **I am chosen for the ultimate inheritance.**

…because of Christ, we have received an inheritance from God, for He chose us from the beginning, and all things happen just as He decided long ago.

Ephesians 1:11 NLT

*

4. **God desired for me to be His child.**

Because of His love God had already decided to make us His own children through Jesus Christ. That is what He wanted and what pleased him.

Ephesians 1:5 NCV

*

5. **I am in the royal family.**

But you are a chosen people, a royal priesthood, a holy nation, a people belonging to God, that you may declare the praises of Him who called you out of darkness into His wonderful light.

I Peter 2:9 NIV

*

6. **I am forgiven.**

…if My people who are called by My name will humble themselves, and pray and seek My face, and turn from their wicked ways, then I will hear from heaven, and will forgive their sin and heal their land.

2 Chronicles 7:14 NKJV

*

7. **I have access to God.**

For through Him we both have access by one Spirit to the Father.

Ephesians 2:18 NKJV

*

8. **I have a divine personal Trainer.**

I will instruct you and guide you along the best pathway for your life; I will advise you and watch your progress.

Psalm 32:8 LB

*

9. **I am promised a bright future.**

I know what I am planning for you, says the Lord. I have good plans for you, not plans to hurt you. I will give you hope and a good future.

Jeremiah 29:11 NCV

*

10. **I have the perfect Guide.**

Trust in the LORD with all your heart, And lean not on your own understanding; In all your ways acknowledge Him, And He shall direct your paths.

Proverbs 3:5-6 NKJV

*

11. **I have the top personal Coach.**

If any of you lacks wisdom, he should ask God who gives generously to all without finding fault, and it will be given to him.

James 1:5 NIV

*

12. **I am the apple of His eye.**

It's in Christ we find out who we are and what we are living for. Long before we first heard of Christ and got our hopes up, he had his eye on us, had designs on us for glorious living.

Ephesians 1:11 The Msg.

*

13. **He cared enough for me to make me trust in Him from the very beginning.**

Yet You brought Me out of the womb; you made Me trust in You even at my mother's breast.

Psalm 22:9 NIV

*

14. **I am a Designer's Original.**

Thank you for making me so wonderfully complex! It is amazing to think about. Your workmanship is marvelous and how well I know it.

Psalm 139:14 LB

*

15. **I am protected by God.**

...He will shield you with His wings. He will shelter you with His feathers. His faithful promises are your armor and protection.

Psalm 91:4 NLT

*

16. **I am complete in Him.**

...and you are complete in Him, who is the head of all principality and power.

Colossians 2:10 NKJV

*

17. **I am not alone.**

Be strong and of good courage, do not be afraid, nor be dismayed, for the LORD your God is with you wherever you go.

Joshua 1:9 NKJV

*

18. **I have 24/7 personal security.**

When you go through deep waters and great trouble, I will be with you. When you go through rivers of difficulty, you will not drown! When you walk through the fire of depression, you will not be burned up …

Isaiah 43:2 LB

*

19. **I cannot be separated from His love.**

For I am persuaded that neither death nor life, nor angels nor principalities nor powers, not things present nor things to come, nor height nor depth, nor any other created thing, shall be able to separate us from the love of God which is in Christ Jesus our Lord.

Romans 8:38-39 NKJV

*

20. **I am assured of God's provision.**

And my God shall supply all your need according to His riches in glory by Christ Jesus.

Philippians 4:19 NKJV

*

21. **I live in great abundance.**

"…I have come that they may have life, and that they may have it more abundantly.

John 10:10 NKJV

*

22. **He sacrificed His life for me.**

I am the good shepherd. The good shepherd gives His life for the sheep.

John 10:11 NKJV

*

23. **I have renewed hope through His word.**

Everything that was written in the past was written to teach us. The Scriptures give us patience and encouragement so that we can have hope.

Romans15:4 NCV

*

24. **I am His top priority.**

God decided to give us life through the word of truth so that we might be the most important of all the things He made.

James1:18 NCV

*

25. **I am God's child.**

But as many as received Him, to them he gave the right to become children of God, to those who believe in His name.

John 1:12 NKJV

*

26. **He cares about every detail.**

Does He not see my ways and count my every step?

Job 31:4 NIV

*

27. **I am designed to live for eternity.**

When this tent we live in – our body here on earth – is torn down, God will have a house in heaven for us to live in, a home he himself has made, which will last forever.

2 Corinthians 5:1 TEV

*

28. **I am crossing over to new beginnings.**

Behold, I will do a new thing. Now it shall spring forth; Shall you not know it? I will even make a road in the wilderness And rivers in the desert.

Isaiah 43:19 NKJV

*

29. **I am able to renew my strength.**

But those who wait on the LORD Shall renew their strength; They shall mount up with wings like eagles. They shall run and not be weary, They shall walk and not faint.

Isaiah 40:31 NKJV

*

30. **I am part of His family.**

Jesus and the people He makes holy all belong to the same family. That is why He isn't ashamed to call them his brothers and sisters.

Hebrews 2:11 CEV

*

31. **I am chosen and appointed by Him.**

You didn't choose me! I appointed you to go and produce lovely fruit always, so that no matter what you ask for from the Father, using my name, he will give it to you.

John 15:16 NKJV

*

32. **I am a vehicle of His love.**

I am the vine, you are the branches. He who abides in Me, and I in him, bears much fruit; for without Me you can do nothing ... If you abide in Me, and My words abide in you, you will ask what you desire, and it shall be done for you.

John 15:5,7 NKJV

*

33. **He is my friend.**

I have called you friends, for all things I have heard from my Father I have made known to you..

John 15:15 NKJV

*

34. **I am trustworthy of His secret.**

God decided to let his people know this rich and glorious secret which He has for all people. This secret is Christ Himself, who is in you. He is our only hope for glory.

Colossians 1:27 NCV

*

35. **I have trust that God will open the doors He has for me.**

The key of the house of David I will lay on his shoulder; So he shall open, and no one shall shut; and he shall shut, and no one shall open."

Isaiah 22:22 NKJV

*

36. **I have a direct line to Him.**

Call to Me, and I will answer you, and show you great and mighty things, which you do not know.

Jeremiah 33:3 NKJV

*

37. **I have ultimate security.**

O Lord, you have examined my heart and know everything about me. You know when I sit or stand. When far away you know my every thought... Every moment you know where I am.

Psalm 139:1-3 LB

*

38. I am content with who I am.

You have no right to argue with your Creator. You are merely a clay pot shaped by a potter. The clay doesn't ask, 'Why did you make me this way?'

Isaiah 45:9 CEV

*

39. I have family responsibilities.

When we have the opportunity to help anyone, we should do it. But we should give special attention to those who are in the family of believers.

Galatians 6:10 NCV

*

40. I belong to God.

For everything, absolutely everything, above and below, visible and invisible, rank after rank of angels – everything got started in him and finds its purpose in him.

Colossians 1:16 The Msg.

*

41. I have a personal 911 line.

The good man does not escape all troubles – he has them too. But the Lord helps him in each and every one.

Psalm 34:19 LB

Chapter 5

I Am Treasured
by His Worth

· ·

*

42. I am His treasure.

Can a mother forget the baby at her breast and have no compassion on the child she has borne? Though she may forget, I will not forget you! See, I have engraved you on the palms of my hands …

Isaiah 49:15-16 NIV

*

43. **I have access to great wealth.**

… whoever accepts and trusts the Son gets in on everything, life complete and forever!

John 3:36 The Msg.

*

44. **I am authentic before Him.**

That's the kind of people the Father is out looking for: those who are simply and honestly themselves before Him in their worship.

John 4:23 The Msg.

*

45. **I am empowered by Him.**

For God has not given us a spirit of fear, but of power and of love and of a sound mind.

2 Timothy 1:7 NKJV

*

46. **I am a friend of God.**

Since we were restored in friendship with God by the death of his Son while we were still His enemies, we will certainly be delivered from eternal punishment by His life.

Romans 5:10 NLT

*

47. I am secure in Him.

I am hidden with Christ in God.

Colossians 3:3 NKJV

*

48. I can be free from conflict.

All this comes from the God who settled the relationship between us and Him, and then called us to settle our relationships with each other.

2 Corinthians 5:18 The Msg.

*

49. I am assured that all things work for my good.

And we know that all things work together for good to those who love God, to those who are the called according to His purpose.

Romans 8:28 NKJV

*

50. I will never be abandoned.

I will never leave you nor forsake you.

Joshua 1:5 NIV

*

51. **I have the privilege of knowing Him.**

I want to know Christ and experience the mighty power that raised him from the dead. I want to suffer with him, sharing in his death,

Philippians 3:10 NLT

*

52. **He shares His secrets with me.**

Friendship with God is reserved for those who reverence Him. With them alone He shares the secrets of his promises.

Psalm 25:14 LB

*

53. **I am free.**

The Lord is the Spirit who gives them life, and where He is there is freedom.

2 Corinthians 3:17 LB

*

54. **I am a citizen of heaven.**

For our citizenship is in heaven, from which we also eagerly wait for the Savior, the Lord Jesus Christ.

Philippians 3:20 NKJV

*

55. I am worth more than fine jewels.

A wife of noble character who can find? She is worth far more than rubies.

Proverbs 31:10 NIV

*

56. I am blessed beyond my wildest dreams.

Glory be to God, who by His mighty power at work within us is able to do far more than we would ever dare to ask or even dream of – infinitely beyond our highest prayers, desires thoughts or hopes.

Ephesians 3:20 LB

*

57. He is available to me.

You will find me when you seek me, if you look for me in earnest.

Jeremiah 29:13 LB

*

58. Mercy and grace are available to me.

Let us therefore come boldly to the throne of grace, that we may obtain mercy and find grace to help in time of need.

Hebrews 4:16 NKJV

*

59. **I am singing a new song.**

He has given me a new song to sing, a hymn of praise to our God. Many will see what He has done and be astounded. They will put their trust in the Lord.

Psalm 40:3 LB

*

60. **God will complete His work in me.**

being confident of this very thing, that He who has begun a good work in you will complete it until the day of Jesus Christ.

Philippians 1:6 NKJV

*

61. **He carries me from instability to stability.**

I waited patiently for God to help me; then He listened and heard my cry. He lifted me out of the pit of despair, ... and set my feet on a hard firm path and steadied me as I walked along.

Psalm 40:1-2 LB

*

62. **I can find strength in quietness.**

... only in returning to me and waiting for me will you be saved; in quietness and confidence is your strength.

Isaiah 30:15 LB

*

63. **I am safe in His arms.**

...he who has been born of God keeps himself, and the wicked one does not touch him.

I John 5:18 NKJV

*

64. **Perfect peace is available for me.**

You, Lord, give perfect peace, to those who keep their purpose firm and put their trust in you.

Isaiah 26:3 TEV

*

65. **I am established, anointed, and sealed by God.**

He anointed us, set his seal of ownership on us, and put his Spirit in our hearts as a deposit, guaranteeing what is to come.

2 Corinthians 1:21-22 NIV

*

66. **When I am fully surrendered, I can enjoy it all.**

I'm asking God for one thing, only one thing: To live with Him in his house my whole life long. I'll contemplate his beauty; I'll study at his feet.

Psalm 27:4 The Msg.

*

67. **God is passionate about me.**

...He is a God who is passionate about His relationship with you.

Exodus 34:14 NLT

*

68. **I can tell Him anything.**

I pour out my complaints before God and tell Him all troubles. For I am overwhelmed ...

Psalm 142:2-3 NLT

*

69. **I am free from condemnation.**

There is therefore now no condemnation to those who are in Christ Jesus, who do not walk according to the flesh, but according to the Spirit.

Romans 8:1-2 NKJV

*

70. **The more I love, the more faith I have.**

The only thing that counts is faith expressing itself through love.

Galatians 5:6 NIV

*

71. **I have found the greatest treasure through His grace.**

But because of His great love for us, God who is rich in mercy, made us alive with Christ even when we were dead in transgressions – it is by grace you have been saved.

Ephesians 2:4-5 NIV

Chapter 6

I Am Competent in His Steps

••

*

72. **The more I persevere, the more mature I become.**

   Perseverance must finish its work so that you may be mature and complete, not lacking anything.

   James 1:4 NIV

*

73. **With His help, I can resist temptation.**

   Watch and pray so that you will not fall into temptation. The spirit is willing, but the body is weak.

   Matthew 26:41 NIV

*

74. **I am chosen to bear fruit.**

You did not choose Me, but I chose you and appointed you that you should go and bear fruit, and that your fruit should remain, that whatever you ask the Father in My Name he may give you.

John 15:16 NKJV

*

75. **Through my weakness I depend on Him.**

When I am weak, then I am strong – the less I have, the more I depend on Christ.

2 Corinthians 12:10 LB

*

76. **I will sparkle in His land when I practice spiritual disciplines.**

Practice (spiritual disciplines). Devote your life to them so that everyone can see our progress.

I Timothy 4:15 GWT

*

77. **I am called to be salt and light in this world.**

You are the salt of the earth; but if the salt loses its flavor, how shall it be seasoned? … You are the light of the world. A city that is set on a hill cannot be hidden…

Matthew 5:13, 14 NKJV

*

78. The spirit of Truth dwells within me.

Do you not know that you are the temple of God and that the Spirit of God dwells in you?

I Corinthians 3:16 NKJV

*

79. I have access to His power.

I pray that out of his glorious riches He may strengthen you with power through His Spirit in your inner being.

Ephesians 3:16 NIV

*

80. The troubles that come my way purify my faith.

These troubles come to prove that your faith is pure. This purity of faith is worth more than gold.

I Peter 1:7 NCV

*

81. When I let God transform my thinking, He gives me clarity.

...let God transform you into a new person by changing the way you think. Then you will know what God wants you to do, and you will know how good and pleasing His will really is.

Romans 12:2b NLT

*

82. **I have been given the privilege to sit next to Him.**

and (He) raised us up together, and made us sit together in the heavenly places in Christ Jesus.

Ephesians 2:6 NKJV

*

83. **My purpose is to do good for His glory.**

For we are His Workmanship, created in Christ Jesus for good works, which God prepared beforehand that we should walk in them.

Ephesians 2:10 NKJV

*

84. **My ultimate goal is to obey Him.**

For God is working in you, giving you the desire to obey him and the power to do what pleases him.

Philippians 2:13 NLT

*

85. **My desire is to be someone that would make God proud.**

Make every effort to give yourself to God as the kind of person He will accept. Be a worker who is not ashamed and who uses the true teaching in the right way.

2 Timothy 2:15 NCV

*

86. I can trust God to do His perfect work in me.

I am sure that God who began the good work within you will keep right on helping you grow in his grace until his task within you is finally finished on that day when Jesus Christ returns.

Philippians 1:6 LB

*

87. My greatest desire is to become like Him.

Our lives gradually become brighter and more beautiful as God enters our lives and we become like Him.

2 Corinthians 3:18 The Msg.

*

88. I have the ability to do all He asks of me.

I can do all things through Christ who strengthens me.

Philippians 4:13 NKJV

*

89. I am dedicated to His divine purpose for me.

Make a careful exploration of who you are and the work you have been given, and then sink yourself into that...

Galatians 6:4 The Msg.

*

90. I have a responsibility to follow the mission He has given me.

Jesus said, In the same way that you, Father, gave me a mission in the world, I give them (my followers) a mission in the world.

John 17:18 The Msg.

*

91. I have the ability to store up treasure for eternity by being generous.

(By being generous and doing good to others) the wealthy in this world will be storing up real treasure for themselves in heaven ... And they will be living a fruitful Christian life down here as well.

I Timothy 6:19 LB

*

92. I have access to His boldness.

In whom we have boldness and access with confidence through faith in Him.

Ephesians 3:12 NKJV

*

93. I have been given the gift of eternal salvation through Christ.

Even though Jesus was the Son of God, He learned obedience by what He suffered. And because His obedience was perfect, He was able to give eternal salvation to all who obey Him.

Hebrews 5:8-9 NCV

*

94. I am given the privilege to work for God.

For we are God's fellow workers; you are God's field, you are God's building.

I Corinthians 3:9 NKJV

*

95. I am focused to receive all God has for me.

Let's keep focused on that goal, those of us who want everything God has for us... God will clear your blurred vision – you'll see it yet!

Philippians 3:15 The Msg.

*

96. I have been given the ministry to reconcile whenever possible.

Now all things are of God who has reconciled us to Himself through Jesus Christ, and has given us the ministry of reconciliation.

2 Corinthians 5:18 NKJV

*

97. I have been given power from above.

But you shall receive power when the Holy Spirit has come upon you; and you shall be witnesses to Me in Jerusalem, and in all Judea and Samaria, and to the end of the earth.

Acts 1:8 NKJV

*

98. I have been given the opportunity to receive the crown of life.

Blessed are those who endure when they are tested. When they pass the test, they will receive the crown of life that God has promised to those who love Him.

James 1:12 GWT

*

99. I am given the gift of ultimate joy through His sacrifice.

Keep your eyes on Jesus, our leader and instructor. He was willing to die a shameful death on the cross because of the joy He knew would be His afterwards.

Hebrews 12:2 LB

*

100. I have access to unlimited mercy and grace.

Let us then approach God's throne of grace with confidence, so that we may receive mercy and find grace to help us in our time of need.

Hebrews 4:16 NIV

*

101. **I have the ability through Christ for ultimate success.**

> He shall be like a tree planted firmly by the rivers of water,
> that brings forth its fruit in its season whose leaf also shall
> not wither; and whatever he does shall prosper.

Psalm 1:3 LB

If you checked the verses you accept and believe in, I congratulate you! Reviewing these truths is the beginning of a new life for you. Now, go back and put a checkmark (with a red pen or pencil) in front of the ones you are actively applying in your life.

Compare your first checks with the red checks. Do you see a pattern? Do you see a gap between what you *believe* in and what you are *acting* on? Write your thoughts.

_____

_____

_____

Brainstorm how you can apply what you now know is available to you. Consider how truths you already have applied to your life have made a difference. If you see a response blocked somehow, examine what has kept you from the application of that particular Truth. Ask yourself, "What is it about these verses that I have a difficult time receiving?" Record your thoughts.

_____

_____

_____

The Truths that weren't checked may have to do with having grown up with a message that is contrary to that particular theme. For example, your view of God may be similar to the view of your earthly father. If you did not have a positive role model as a father, it may be more difficult to accept these Truths. If that is the case I encourage you to talk with your Heavenly Father. Just be honest and tell Him your conflict. He knows anyway, but He wants you to express yourself. If you are angry, let Him know. He is big enough to handle your anger. Pour out your heart to God. Ask Him to help you forgive yourself for not trusting His Word. Then ask Him to help you trust and accept His deep love for you. I also encourage you to talk to a trusted Christian friend, your pastor, a professional counselor, or someone else who could help you in this area. Don't put it off. You can turn your life around from victim to victor for the rest of your life.

Dear Heavenly Father,

We thank you and praise you for the awesome God that you are. It is difficult for _____ to grasp how deep your love is for her. We know that sometimes it feels safer to remain a victim because it is familiar. We also know that that position is satan's trap, so I pray that _____ would no longer be comfortable there. Give _____ the discipline to claim your Word everyday, the courage to stand firm against the enemy, and the strength to fight the spiritual battle, because You have said, "Therefore submit to God. Resist the devil and he will flee from you." (James 4:7) Help _____ to humbly submit to you, to resist the devil with your Word and to thank you that satan doesn't have a chance … so he must flee.

In Jesus' name,
Amen.

Part 3

STEPPING UP TO CHAMPIONSHIP

Chapter 7

Know Your True Identity

....

Knowing your true identity in Christ includes believing and accepting the Truths on which you just meditated. Since nothing is more powerful than grasping your true identity, the benefits of knowing it—*really* knowing it—are priceless. Below are listed twenty-five such benefits, and this list is only a beginning. As you develop an awareness of who you are in Christ, the benefits become innumerable. Feel free to add to the list and make it your own.

Knowing your true identity in Christ will:

- open new doors.
- take you to places you never dreamed of going.
- open opportunities to be ecstatic about the highs and peaceful about the lows.
- allow you to respect and find beauty in little things.

- develop a deeper desire and delight in big things.
- give you the courage to cross over to new beginnings.
- help you take more risks.
- increase your focus.
- strengthen you and keep you from growing weary.
- increase your confidence.
- take your faith to higher levels.
- develop greater boldness.
- give you deeper love.
- increase your stability.
- allow you greater contentment.
- give you deeper peace.
- protect you from jealousy and other negative influences.
- increase your optimism and sense of gratitude.
- give you greater hope.
- remind you that you are not alone.
- grant you deeper rest.
- increase your laughter.
- give you deeper appreciation for your family.
- increase your gratitude for the stories of previous generations.
- help you discover blessings all around you.

Chapter 8

Claim Your Identity in Christ

....

*Y*our identity in Christ allows you access to everything Christ is and what He does for you. The contrary is also true. If you do not have a sense of who you are in Christ—or at least not a strong sense—you will find that for each positive area listed above, you can come up with a negative. For example, I mentioned insecurity. When you feel insecure, you may hang on to negatives messages that feed your insecurity. These may sound like "*I could never do that.*" "*It sounds good, but I have tried those programs, and they don't work for me.*" Or perhaps you hear an inner message like, "*She always gets all the breaks. It sure would be nice if someone did something for me.*"

These particular responses often whirl around in the mind of someone who has been hurt in some way. As a result, discouragement floods in. It is natural for us to face discouragement from time to time. The difference lies in how we respond to it.

Let's say you are part of my class. I ask for a volunteer who has been discouraged lately to join me at the front of the class. You volunteer. When you come up, I ask you to share with the group what your discouragement feels like. Not what is *making* you discouraged, but what the discouragement *feels* like to you. So you do.

Then I ask for four more volunteers, this time two people who know you well and two who do not. I ask these volunteers to share with you (and the class) the strengths they see in you. They may share some things you already know about yourself, or they may share some things you don't know about yourself. Perhaps you have forgotten some of these traits.

My question would then be, "How do you feel now?"

When four people have just empowered you—especially publicly—with bold statements about your strengths, you cannot help but feel good about yourself. The only way you would not feel good is if you did not receive—not just acknowledge, but *receive*—what they were saying. Here is the key: your discouragement can turn to more courage when you remember what your strengths are. When you know who you are in Christ and walk in your strengths, *nobody* has the power to take you down unless you allow him the opportunity. Paula White, Christian evangelist, teacher, television personality, and author says, "No one can mess with me on the outside if I know who I am on the inside."

It's only when you give others—or the devil—permission to put negative thoughts in your mind *and you entertain those thoughts* that you lose ground and get discouraged. As a believer, remember who you are in Christ. **Knowing this is the most powerful tool that exists.** It will allow you to break through anything that is holding you back. If you know and believe that your security is in Him, you can confidently say along with Paul the Apostle, "*For I can do everything through Christ, who gives me strength*" (Philippians 4:13 NLT).

Dear Heavenly Father,

We thank you that you have made a way so we can have access to an identity with you. Help _____ to remember that every time he gets discouraged to immediately stop and claim his identity in you. All _____ has to do is go back to one of your promises and claim it. It almost seems too good to be true, Lord, but we thank you that you have made what is seemingly impossible, possible. Thanks for your great love and faithfulness in our lives.

In Jesus' name,
Amen.

Chapter 9

Turn It Around

....

Before change will occur, three things must happen.

First, previous unhealthy thought patterns must be broken. Remember, most difficulties begin with mindset and belief systems. If you don't know who you are, you may feel insecure, focus on the negative, believe you can't move forward, or feel hopelessly stuck and defeated. If you experience any of these, note the first trigger. What was happening when you first began to be discouraged? Perhaps something didn't go your way? Did someone not meet your expectations? Were you hurt by an unkind remark? Rather than to buckle under in self-pity, humbly give it over to God *every time* it happens. Submitting to Him is where your real power lies. Humility is the key. Self-pity just leads to more discouragement, eventually driving away those who may be positioned to help you. You must give up self-pity—a poor-me attitude—in order to come to God humbly. Remember, you must give up so that you can go up.

Second, choose to change. Once you are aware of any pattern that takes you to discouragement, do something about it. Even if you experience negative emotions, you have the ability and power to change. It really is a choice. Don't wait until a major crisis happens and then decide to change. Decide now to do whatever it takes to alter your thinking or you may continue to miss out on what God has for you. If you have a relationship with Jesus Christ, ask Him to forgive you for not trusting Him, for not fully realizing what is available to you. Let Him know you desire His help in experiencing and enjoying all He has for you.

Third, replace negative messages with positive ones. Part of remembering who you are in Christ is centering your thoughts on Truth. Practical tips and tools are available that will help you get started with this change. You will find them in the section *Stepping up to Championship.*

Dear Heavenly Father,

Thank you that you see every tear we cry.

You know how much _____ wants to turn things around, yet she so often gets caught up in old patterns. Please help _____ to review your promises over and over again until she fully grasps your power to help her overcome any challenge that comes her way.

In Jesus' name,
Amen.

Chapter 10

Recognize the Favor on Your Life

· ·

*L*et's visit a story that happened more than two thousand years ago. It is a story that is still told and celebrated every year, a story you may have often heard yourself. But let's look at it from a different perspective. This is the story of the birth of Jesus Christ, as found in the gospel of Luke, the second chapter.

Mary, the mother of Jesus, may have been the most unlikely young woman to be chosen to bear the Christ child. Considered to be about fifteen or sixteen years of age, she was leaving childhood, but she had not yet fully completed her journey into adulthood. Some people today would consider this time of life a prime time for an identity crisis. What would she know about being a wife? How would she know how to raise a child when she was scarcely out of childhood herself? Would she know how to sacrificially love a baby at all, let alone if that baby were the Son of God? So, why would God choose her for this highly honored position?

He chose her because she had all the traits of a true champion. God saw an obedient and vulnerable heart. God saw that Mary was willing to follow and believe the impossible even when she didn't understand. God saw her willingness to walk into the unknown, even at the price of her own reputation. And God saw that the young Jewish girl was bold and courageous, willing to step out in faith and go where no one had ever been asked to go before. Yet Mary's heart was peaceful. She was content with just knowing the next step. God knew she would be loyal and faithful because she had a tender heart towards Him.

When the angel Gabriel appeared to Mary, his first words were, *"Rejoice, highly favored one."* He was bringing good news to someone who was honored. Then he says, *"...the Lord is with you; blessed are you among women."* Gabriel states here two important things we must know as champions: 1) who we are in Christ, and 2) we are never alone. In his initial statement, Gabriel assured Mary of both these truths.

Since she was being addressed by a stranger, Mary's initial response of fear would have been normal and natural. Luke puts it this way: *"...she was troubled at his saying, and considered what manner of greeting this was."*

The angel responded. *"Do not be afraid, Mary, for you have found favor with God."* In these first statements, Gabriel assured Mary several times that she was favored by God. It was the most important thing Mary needed to know. God wanted to be sure Mary knew her true identity. If she could grasp her true identity—that she was favored by God and that she would never be alone—she would be able to face and break through whatever came along. He was laying the foundation for great success.

Now he was ready to give her the assignment, the reason he was sent by God. He proceeded, *"And, behold, you will conceive in your womb and bring forth a Son and shall call His name JESUS."*

The angel told Mary she would conceive, and he also informed her of the news that her cousin Elizabeth had also conceived in her old age. Gabriel concludes his message with the declaration *"For with God nothing will be impossible."*

Now listen to Mary's response: *"Behold the maidservant of the Lord! Let it be to me according to your word."* Mary *received* the message the angel had brought, and she consciously made the decision to be obedient to a high calling. And, as soon as Gabriel *received* Mary's word of obedience, his assignment was complete. He departed.

It is no different for you and me. We *must* know who we are in Christ. When we grasp our true identity in Christ and believe that we are never alone, we too will be able to face every challenge that comes our way and we will break through to victory.

Each one of us is given an assignment. We know this by what John says in his gospel when he quotes Jesus (John 15:16). *"You did not choose Me, but I chose you and appointed you that you should go and bear fruit, and that your fruit should remain, that whatever you ask the Father in My name He may give you."* That appointment, friends, is huge. Just as God trusted Mary with an awesome assignment, He trusts you with an awesome assignment. If you will accept His favor, you too will conceive … you will conceive and birth unimaginable dreams and passions that run deep in your heart.

"For with God nothing will be impossible."

Have you given up on your dreams? Have you even allowed yourself to dream at all? Regardless of your situation, God opens new doors continually, desiring to fulfill the very dreams He has placed in your heart. He has been preparing you all this time; now He is waiting to see your obedient heart. As you delight in Him, He will give you the desires of your heart. God's promise is echoed by David's words in Psalm 37:4, *"Delight yourself also in the* LORD, *and He shall give you the desires of your heart."* This is God's promise, and He will fulfill it.

Dear Heavenly Father,

Thank you for the opportunities that you give us.

I pray you would give _____ the heart of Mary, a heart obedient to the call to do the impossible, to follow the unknown, to leave everything familiar in order to go into the unknown. Help _____ to remember that she is highly favored. Just as you were there for Mary, you are there for her. Help _____ to remember you are the God of impossibilities. Thank you for wanting to fulfill _____'s dream.

In Jesus' name,
Amen

Chapter 11

Break Through to Championship

∙∙

*G*od chose you. He loved you from before you were born, and He has invited you to be part of His family. Whether you believe it or not, you are His champion. You may not act like a champion. You may not even feel like a champion. But if you begin doing the exercises in this book, you will begin *thinking* like a champion and that's where it all starts.

Because we are bombarded daily with messages in society that are contrary to our true worth, it is important that we remind ourselves *daily* who we are in Christ. If we don't, we lose perspective quickly and miss out on all the promises that are available to us. To become champions, we must practice when we feel like it and practice when we don't. Living to our full potential requires a huge cost, but the result is worth everything we invest.

Let's look at some practical tools to help you in your journey. Focus on one exercise every day for two to three weeks before going on to another. Remember, who you are in Christ is the most powerful concept you can ever learn.

1. Choose a verse from the list under *Reaching Higher*. Look in the mirror each morning and say, "Did anyone ever tell you how beautiful you are?" Then, in response to that question, read your chosen verse. You might reply to yourself, "Yes! God, in Psalms139, says that I am fearfully and wonderfully made." Choose a different verse each week.

Dear Heavenly Father,

Thank you that you have created beauty all around us.

Please help _____ to know how beautiful she is. You have created the beauty from deep within to shine through to the outside. Help _____ to remember that every genuine smile, every kind word, every good deed does not go unnoticed by you.

In Jesus' name,
Amen.

2. Choose one title from *101 Truths to a Powerful You* on which to meditate each week. Hold a small hand mirror to where you can only see your eyes. (If a small mirror is unavailable, simply cover your face below your eyes with a piece of paper.) Every day say the truth five times, emphasizing a

different word with each repetition. It may feel awkward at first, but do it sincerely to bring new meaning to the Truth. For example:

I am the apple of His eye.

I AM the apple of His eye.

I am the APPLE of His eye.

I am the apple of HIS eye.

I am the apple of His EYE.

Dear Heavenly Father,

Thank you that we are the apple of your eye. You have designed us and had your eye on us long before we were even born. Help _____ to remember this truth, especially when she faces difficult times. As _____ does this exercise, may she receive the message deep into her heart.

In Jesus' name,
Amen.

3. Create specific movements to illustrate a specific Truth or verse. Consider learning the verse in sign language, or make up your own movements to kinesthetically remember the words. Practice the moves every day, preferably as part of your morning routine. You might swing one arm saying, "I am the apple of His eye", swing the other arm and say, "I am fearfully and wonderfully made." Then swing them together and declare, "I am a Designer's child." Memory is tied to movement, so this is especially fun to do with young children.

Dear Heavenly Father,

Thank you for the many ways you let us know that you love us. Today is a new day, a day that will allow _____ on a new journey of deeper insight, deeper love, and deeper faith. Thank you for making that possible. Help _____ to find special promises to help him remember how personal your love is for him.

In Jesus' name,
Amen.

4. Enlarge a photograph that reminds you of a favorite verse. Write the truth and verse on the mat or separate piece of cardstock. Frame and position it in a prominent place to remind you of positive memories and important truths that bring new worship to your soul.

Dear Heavenly Father,

You have given us so much and we are so grateful that your mercies are new every morning. Thank you that just as you asked the people in the Old Testament to choose things that reminded them of what you did for them, we can also find photos or tangible things to remind us of what you have done for us. Remind _____ to take photos that will inspire her in her daily walk with You.

In Jesus' name,
Amen

Chapter 12

Become Part of a Bigger Family

· ·

*G*od has extended to us an invitation to join His family. If you have not accepted this invitation, or you are not sure if you are a part of the family of God, I encourage you to read the following and then pray the prayer. Doing so will be the best decision you will ever make.

1. **God loves us.** In fact the Bible says that God loves us so much that He gave His only Son so that we can experience eternal life with Him. God *willingly* sacrificed His only Son, Jesus, for *us*. How did this happen?

2. **Sin separates us from God**. Sin may be wrongful thoughts, attitudes, or actions. The wages, or payment, for the sin we have committed is death—God says so in Romans 6:23

"For the wages of sin is death…" It's what we deserve. But this is the best part, the gift of God. God sent His only Son to die *for* us. He actually took our place. In obedience, Jesus willingly went to the cross, not because He had done anything wrong, but so that the penalty for *our* sins might be paid, that our sins might be forgiven. In doing this, God showed his great love for us.

> *"For God so loved the world that He gave us His only Son, that whosoever believes in Him should not perish but have eternal life"* (John 3:16).

Love doesn't get any bigger than that.

3. **God offers each of us the gift of eternal life**. Paul the Apostle says it this way:

> *"The wages of sin is death but the gift of God is eternal life through Jesus Christ our Lord"* (Romans 6:23).

Gifts are free; eternal life is a *free* gift.

4. **We accept salvation like we receive any other gift**. We have a say in the matter. All we need to do to become a part of the family of God is to be sorry for our sins (this is called repentance), believe in our hearts that God sent His only Son to die for us and that He rose again (this is called faith). And then receive this gift through prayer (this is called salvation).

If we accept the gift of eternal life, we will spend eternity with Him in heaven and enjoy His presence here with us on earth. We become part of the family of God.

> "*But as many as received Him, to them He gave the right to become children of God, to those who believe in His name*" (John 1:12).

5. **Pray this prayer,** if this expresses the desire of your heart.

Dear Heavenly Father,

I'm sorry for my sin—for all my wrong attitudes, actions, and thoughts. Please forgive me. Thank you that your love is big enough to cover everything. Thank you for the special gift of sending your Son to die for me. Thank you that He rose from the dead. I accept this gift, and I invite you into my life. I am excited to begin a new relationship with you.

In Jesus' name,
Amen.

If you prayed this prayer, welcome to the family of God! You are forgiven and will some day live forever with Jesus in Heaven. How exciting!

As in any family, it is the beginning of new relationships, new adventures, and new responsibilities. God has given us the Bible (His Word), which tells us all about each of these areas and much, much more. As a new member of His family, get to know other believers and learn more about your new life in Christ by regularly attending a Bible-believing church. If you do not have a Bible, ask the pastor where you can get one, or purchase one at a local Christian bookstore. Begin reading the Gospel of John. Share your decision with someone who is a part of God's family. Consider telling the pastor or his wife.

I am so happy for you! I invite you to email me or write me a note telling me about your decision. I would consider it a privilege to pray for you.

May God bless you richly in every way!

THE NEXT STEP

As you read this book and go through the exercises my prayer for you is that this book would become a handbook for you, one that you can continually refer back to and meditate on His promises. I pray that you would be open to growth and remember that with direct access to God, you can defeat any battle or challenge that comes your way.

Are you ready for more? Would you like to get beyond the frustration of living a mundane life and become the Champion you were meant to be?

I can help.

————➤✦◄————

Have you ever looked into the mirror and wondered who you are staring at? Have you ever wondered why are you on this earth? What if you displayed the qualities of a Champion where-ever you went and anyone in the world would stop and listen?

It doesn't matter where you are in life, you can choose to become a Champion. The best place to start is to reread through the book if you have already read it. Now, use the tools I have outlined for you. You will be amazed at what you learn about yourself. In addition, I have offered additional resources and tools in the back of the book. I encourage you to go through them as well.

You will not want to miss our fabulous 2-day Story Retreat. It is two full days of fun, interaction and story time. For more information go to www.wealththroughstories.com/story-retreat.

If you would like more of a hands-on Coaching program and be part of a community, I invite you to go to www.wealththroughstories.com and sign up for a complimentary Story Strategy session to find out how you can get involved.

Just remember, every step will take you closer to loving your story and becoming the Champion you were meant to be.

About the Author

....

*L*inda *A Olson* provides Story Coaching for future storytellers through her successful *Wealth Through Stories* program. With more than forty years of leadership experience, she expertly helps entrepreneurs, business owners, coaches and authors, break through perceived barriers to discover their stories for maximum impact. As a speaker, Linda captivates audiences with engaging storytelling and thought-provoking questions. As a trainer, Linda inspires and motivates her clients to learn quickly and remember more so that they can utilize valuable skills both personally and professionally. As an International Amazon #1 Bestselling author, Linda thrives on helping others to see value in their own stories in order to impact the world and to grow their own businesses. She says it like this:

> "*I take your life-experience*
> *and turn it into the transformation of lives*
> *by helping you find power and wealth in your story.*"

Wealth Through Stories

"IMPACTING MILLIONS THROUGH STORY"

Own Your Story Before It Owns You

5 Steps to Freedom

"IMPACTING MILLIONS THROUGH STORY"

by Linda A. Olson

Go to http://wealththroughstories.com/
trust-5-keys-gift to pick up your FREE gift.

TRUST

5 Keys to Finding
Your Story That Can
Impact Millions

by LINDA A. OLSON

Wealth through Stories
GREAT STORYTELLERS. GREAT SPEAKERS. GREAT BUSINESS.

Go to www.wealththroughstories.com
to pick up your copy.

What are you really offering?

5 Simple steps using story
To attract more customers
by LINDA A. OLSON

Wealth through Stories
GREAT STORYTELLERS. GREAT SPEAKERS. GREAT BUSINESS.

© 2016 Linda Olson and Wealth Through Stories | www.wealththroughstories.com

To receive your copy go to
https://wealththroughstories.com/breakthrough

BREAKTHROUGH

5 Simple Steps
To Letting Go of the Past

Linda A. Olson

Wealth Through Stories
"IMPACTING MILLIONS THROUGH STORY"

———⟶⟨⟩———

Go to https://wealththroughstories/goliath
to receive your tool on defeating your goliath.

DEFEATING YOUR GOLIATH

Learn to use a simple tool

To defeat your goliath

in

Seven days or less.

5 - DAY CHALLENGE ON
CREATING A STORY
THAT TRANSFORMS
From Potential Lead To Client

Wealth Through Stories
"IMPACTING MILLIONS THROUGH STORY"

Learn the 5 Keys to
going from not being
sure you have a
STORY...

$197
$17

...to creating a
transformational
story inside our
5-day
challenge.

✓ How to be CONFIDENT you have a story

✓ Where to find the BEST story to reach your tribe

✓ How your story can be the SOLUTION

✓ The secret to CONNECTING through story

✓ TRANSFORM a potential lead to becoming a client

Sources

··

1 Adapted from several sources and revised: *www. CharacterThatCounts, Developing the Leader Within You by* John Maxwell, Definitions from the Apple, Inc.

Why different Translations? Every translation has its limitations. My goal is to help you receive as much clarity as possible. Another reason is if we have memorized or are familiar with particular verses they lose their meaning when we continually repeat them the same way. A new translation brings freshness and newness and deeper insight.

Scripture marked CEV is taken from the *Contemporary English Version*. Copyright 1995 by the American Bible Society, New York, NY. Used by permission.